MATH SERIES

Word Problems

Book Two

by H. S. Lawrence

Book design by Kifer Graphics

Thanks to:
Laurie Hoffman, Cody Hoffman, and Kayla Hoffman

Published by:
Garlic Press
605 Powers St.
Eugene, OR 97402

ISBN 0-931993-42-3
Order Number GP-042

ww.garlicpress.com

Contents

Word Problems, Book 2

Word Problems, Book 2 is a continuation of the earlier *Word Problems, Book 1* which focused only on addition and subtraction skills needed to solve word problems.

Word Problems, Book 2 extends the word problems skills needed to solve multiplication and division problems. Again, like Book 1, *The 4 Step Model* is presented from which word problems using addition, subtraction, multiplication or division can be solved.

Simple operational skills for advanced addition, advanced subtraction, advanced multiplication, division, and decimals are tested prior to working with formal word problems. With these skills firm, their use in the word problems that follow prove much easier.

In addition to *The 4 Step Model*, additional word problem skills are taught: Finding Extra Information; Problems with Several Steps; and work with signs, charts, and graphs.

A Post Test section allows for an assessment of acquired skills. And an Answer Section provides answers to all problems presented.

Advanced Addition Review

$$
\begin{array}{r} 27 \\ +\ 48 \\ \hline \end{array}
\longrightarrow
\begin{array}{r} {}^{1}27 \\ +\ 48 \\ \hline 5 \end{array}
\longrightarrow
\begin{array}{r} {}^{1}27 \\ +\ 48 \\ \hline 75 \end{array}
\longrightarrow
\begin{array}{r} 27 \\ +\ 48 \\ \hline 75 \end{array}
$$

Solve the addition problems below.

5 7 + 1 8	2 3 + 2 7	2 5 + 3 5	1 4 + 1 9	4 7 + 2 9	1 5 + 2 5
1 2 1 6 + 1 5	3 4 2 2 + 3 4	1 6 1 3 + 1 7	1 5 6 5 + 1 3	2 6 1 6 + 2 6	4 5 2 9 + 1 2
1 9 + 3 4	5 6 + 3 6	3 9 + 1 9	4 8 + 2 3	2 5 + 1 8	1 9 + 1 6
2 4 1 5 + 1 2	3 8 1 1 + 3 8	1 4 2 2 + 2 6	1 5 2 3 + 3 2	1 6 1 1 + 1 6	2 4 4 2 + 1 7
2 8 + 6 2	1 7 + 1 9	2 7 + 1 5	1 7 + 4 7	2 6 + 3 6	2 5 + 2 6

Advanced Subtraction Review

$$
\begin{array}{r} 54 \\ -\ 37 \\ \hline \end{array}
\quad\longrightarrow\quad
\begin{array}{r} {}^{4}\!5^{1}4 \\ -\ 37 \\ \hline 7 \end{array}
\quad\longrightarrow\quad
\begin{array}{r} {}^{4}5^{1}4 \\ -\ 37 \\ \hline 17 \end{array}
\quad\longrightarrow\quad
\begin{array}{r} 54 \\ -\ 37 \\ \hline 17 \end{array}
$$

Solve the subtraction problems below.

8 1 − 2 2	6 4 − 3 9	9 5 − 4 8	8 6 − 4 9	8 2 − 1 9	7 1 − 2 6
8 5 − 2 6	7 1 − 3 8	5 4 − 1 9	7 2 − 1 7	9 5 − 4 8	6 1 − 4 3
7 6 − 1 8	9 1 − 2 4	6 2 − 2 7	9 1 − 1 8	7 3 − 4 9	8 7 − 1 8
9 1 − 7 9	8 6 − 6 9	4 3 − 1 7	8 2 − 1 6	5 1 − 2 2	9 5 − 3 9
6 5 − 1 9	9 3 − 1 8	8 1 − 6 9	7 2 − 3 8	8 2 − 1 7	4 2 − 1 9

Advanced Multiplication Review

$$
\begin{array}{r} 26 \\ \times\,2 \\ \hline \end{array}
\longrightarrow
\begin{array}{r} \overset{1}{2}6 \\ \times\,2 \\ \hline 2 \end{array}
\longrightarrow
\begin{array}{r} \overset{1}{2}6 \\ \times\,2 \\ \hline 52 \end{array}
\longrightarrow
\begin{array}{r} 26 \\ \times\,2 \\ \hline 52 \end{array}
$$

Solve the multiplication problems below.

1 8 x 3	1 5 x 5	2 3 x 4	1 4 x 5	4 9 x 2	2 8 x 3
3 3 x 8	7 2 x 6	6 5 x 3	9 7 x 9	1 8 x 6	8 5 x 4
3 6 x 2	2 6 x 3	4 7 x 5	1 5 x 7	1 9 x 8	1 3 x 7
5 3 x 5	8 6 x 7	5 7 x 2	9 5 x 6	8 6 x 9	7 5 x 4
1 9 x 2	1 6 x 4	2 4 x 6	4 5 x 5	2 8 x 3	3 7 x 8

$6 \div 2 =$

Division Review

Solve the division problems below.

1	**2**	**3**	**4**
$18 \div 3 =$	$25 \div 5 =$	$18 \div 6 =$	$21 \div 7 =$
$33 \div 3 =$	$60 \div 5 =$	$60 \div 6 =$	$56 \div 7 =$
$27 \div 3 =$	$10 \div 5 =$	$24 \div 6 =$	$14 \div 7 =$
$36 \div 3 =$	$40 \div 5 =$	$66 \div 6 =$	$70 \div 7 =$
$21 \div 3 =$	$35 \div 5 =$	$6 \div 6 =$	$7 \div 7 =$
$24 \div 3 =$	$20 \div 5 =$	$72 \div 6 =$	$84 \div 7 =$
$12 \div 4 =$	$55 \div 5 =$	$48 \div 6 =$	$28 \div 7 =$
$32 \div 4 =$	$5 \div 5 =$	$30 \div 6 =$	$77 \div 7 =$
$48 \div 4 =$	$45 \div 5 =$	$54 \div 6 =$	$35 \div 7 =$
$28 \div 4 =$	$30 \div 5 =$	$36 \div 6 =$	$49 \div 7 =$
$36 \div 4 =$	$15 \div 5 =$	$42 \div 6 =$	$63 \div 7 =$
$24 \div 4 =$	$50 \div 5 =$	$12 \div 6 =$	$42 \div 7 =$

5	**6**	**7**	**8**
$32 \div 8 =$	$90 \div 9 =$	$80 \div 10 =$	$60 \div 12 =$
$80 \div 8 =$	$27 \div 9 =$	$110 \div 10 =$	$120 \div 12 =$
$24 \div 8 =$	$108 \div 9 =$	$90 \div 10 =$	$24 \div 12 =$
$72 \div 8 =$	$18 \div 9 =$	$120 \div 10 =$	$96 \div 12 =$
$8 \div 8 =$	$54 \div 9 =$	$70 \div 10 =$	$132 \div 12 =$
$96 \div 8 =$	$81 \div 9 =$	$100 \div 10 =$	$36 \div 12 =$
$16 \div 8 =$	$9 \div 9 =$	$77 \div 11 =$	$108 \div 12 =$
$88 \div 8 =$	$72 \div 9 =$	$121 \div 11 =$	$12 \div 12 =$
$64 \div 8 =$	$36 \div 9 =$	$110 \div 11 =$	$144 \div 12 =$
$48 \div 8 =$	$99 \div 9 =$	$55 \div 11 =$	$48 \div 12 =$
$40 \div 8 =$	$45 \div 9 =$	$132 \div 11 =$	$84 \div 12 =$
$56 \div 8 =$	$63 \div 9 =$	$99 \div 11 =$	$72 \div 12 =$

Adding and Subtracting Decimals

Line up the decimal point before adding or subtracting.

Add .24 + 1.7:

incorrect
```
 .24
+1.7
```

correct
```
 .24
+1.7
```

$\longrightarrow$
```
 .24
+1.7
─────
   4
```

$\longrightarrow$
```
 .24
+1.7
─────
  94
```

$\longrightarrow$
```
  .24
+ 1.7
─────
1 9.4
```

The decimal points all line up.

```
  1.17          .61         3.05         7.17          .59
+  .52       +2.80        +2.32        + .08        +3.98
─────        ──────       ──────       ──────       ──────
```

```
  7.63         6.11         6.73         8.37         4.03
-  .88       -5.22        -2.2         -5.41        -1.02
─────        ──────       ──────       ──────       ──────
```

Line up the decimal points before adding.

2.44 + 3.6 =   1.00 + 4.39 =   .7 + .07 =

.81 + 6.26 =   5.56 + 7.3 =   4 + .27 =

Line up the decimal points before subtracting.

5.27 − .35 =   1.63 − .9 =   4.8 − 3.28 =

2.55 − .334 =   36.1 − 3.62 =   .99 − .244 =

Multiplying Decimals Review

Example 1

$$\begin{array}{r} 1.23 \\ \times\ 2 \\ \hline \end{array} \longrightarrow \begin{array}{r} 1.23 \\ \times\ 2 \\ \hline 6 \end{array} \longrightarrow \begin{array}{r} 1.23 \\ \times\ 2 \\ \hline 46 \end{array} \longrightarrow \begin{array}{r} 1.23 \\ \times\ 2 \\ \hline 246 \end{array} \longrightarrow \begin{array}{r} 1.23 \\ \times\ 2 \\ \hline 2.46 \end{array}$$

Example 2

$$\begin{array}{r} 1.23 \\ \times\ .2 \\ \hline \end{array} \longrightarrow \begin{array}{r} 1.23 \\ \times\ .2 \\ \hline 6 \end{array} \longrightarrow \begin{array}{r} 1.23 \\ \times\ .2 \\ \hline 46 \end{array} \longrightarrow \begin{array}{r} 1.23 \\ \times\ .2 \\ \hline 246 \end{array} \longrightarrow \begin{array}{r} 1.23 \\ \times\ .2 \\ \hline .246 \end{array}$$

$\begin{array}{r} 3.7 \\ \times\ 6 \\ \hline \end{array}$	$\begin{array}{r} 8.2 \\ \times\ .4 \\ \hline \end{array}$	$\begin{array}{r} .37 \\ \times\ .5 \\ \hline \end{array}$	$\begin{array}{r} 4.2 \\ \times\ 6 \\ \hline \end{array}$	$\begin{array}{r} .18 \\ \times\ .7 \\ \hline \end{array}$
$\begin{array}{r} 2.4 \\ \times\ 7 \\ \hline \end{array}$	$\begin{array}{r} 66 \\ \times\ .5 \\ \hline \end{array}$	$\begin{array}{r} .42 \\ \times\ 4 \\ \hline \end{array}$	$\begin{array}{r} .36 \\ \times\ .8 \\ \hline \end{array}$	$\begin{array}{r} 2.4 \\ \times\ 9 \\ \hline \end{array}$
$\begin{array}{r} .86 \\ \times\ 5 \\ \hline \end{array}$	$\begin{array}{r} 3.4 \\ \times\ .3 \\ \hline \end{array}$	$\begin{array}{r} 1.7 \\ \times\ 5 \\ \hline \end{array}$	$\begin{array}{r} .02 \\ \times\ .9 \\ \hline \end{array}$	$\begin{array}{r} 9.3 \\ \times\ 2 \\ \hline \end{array}$
$\begin{array}{r} 1.4 \\ \times\ .3 \\ \hline \end{array}$	$\begin{array}{r} 6.1 \\ \times\ 7 \\ \hline \end{array}$	$\begin{array}{r} 7.6 \\ \times\ 2 \\ \hline \end{array}$	$\begin{array}{r} .38 \\ \times\ 4 \\ \hline \end{array}$	$\begin{array}{r} 5.7 \\ \times\ .9 \\ \hline \end{array}$

The 4 Step Model:

Step 1. Read the Problem.

Read the problem. <u>Underline what the problem is asking.</u>

Like this

Joey has 22 comic books. He will give 17 of them to his younger brother Troy. <u>How many will he still have left?</u>

Katrina recycles soda cans. She recycled 36 cans last month. This month she recycled 34 cans. <u>How many total cans did she recycle?</u>

Bradley mailed 22 birthday party invitations. Only 18 friends came to his party. How many friends did not come?

Pam made fruit salad. She cut a watermelon into 57 pieces. She cut a cantaloupe into 38 pieces. She cut a honeydew melon into 41 pieces. How many pieces of fruit were in the fruit salad altogether?

Jake is 4 years old. His brother, John, is 4 times as old as Jake. How old is John?

Ramona is going to the carnival. She has $10.00 to buy ride tickets. Each ride ticket costs $2.00. How many ride tickets will she be able to buy?

Read the problem. <u>Underline</u> what the problem is asking.

Step 2. Find the Facts.

(Circle) the facts that will answer the problem.

Like this

(Joey has 22 comic books.) He will give 17 of them to his younger brother Troy.) How many will he still have left?

Katrina recycles soda cans. (She recycled 36 cans last month.) (This month she recycled 34 cans.) How many total cans did she recycle?

Bradley mailed 22 birthday party invitations. Only 18 friends came to his party. How many friends did not come?

Pam made fruit salad. She cut a watermelon into 57 pieces. She cut a cantaloupe into 38 pieces. She cut a honeydew melon into 41 pieces. How many pieces of fruit were in the fruit salad altogether?

Jake is 4 years old. His brother, John, is 4 times as old as Jake. How old is John?

Ramona is going to the carnival. She has $10.00 to buy ride tickets. Each ride ticket costs $2.00. How many ride tickets will she be able to buy?

Read the problem. <u>Underline</u> what the problem is asking.
Find the facts. (Circle) the facts that will answer the problem.

Step 3. Find the Operation.

Box key words that help solve the problem

Like this

Joey has 22 comic books. He will give 17 of them to his younger brother Troy. How many will he still have left?

Key words can be helpful. Be careful! Some problems may not have key words.	**Addition**	**Subtraction**	**Multiplication**	**Division**
	additional	difference	times	each
	in all	left	in all	equal
	altogether	take away	total	per
	total	only	each	separate
	all	more than		
	another	less than		

Katrina recycles soda cans. She recycled 36 cans last month. This month she recycled 34 cans. How many total cans did she recycle?

Bradley mailed 22 birthday party invitations. Only 18 friends came to his party. How many friends did not come?

Pam made fruit salad. She cut a watermelon into 57 pieces. She cut a cantaloupe into 38 pieces. She cut a honeydew melon into 41 pieces. How many pieces of fruit were in the fruit salad altogether?

Jake is 4 years old. His brother, John, is 4 times as old as Jake. How old is John?

Ramona is going to the carnival. She has $10.00 to buy ride tickets. Each ride ticket costs $2.00. How many ride tickets will she be able to buy?

Step 4. Work the Problem.

Use the correct facts and the correct operation to work these problems. Label the answer.

Joey has 22 comic books. He will give 17 of them to his younger brother Troy. How many will he still have left?

Like this ➡

$$\begin{array}{r} 2\overset{1}{2} \\ -\ 17 \\ \hline \end{array}$$

5 comic books

Fact: Joey has 22 comic books.
Fact: He will give 17 of them to his younger brother Troy.
Operation: Subtraction
Key words: left

Key Words

Addition
additional
in all
altogether
total
all
another

Subtraction
difference
left
take away
only
more than
less than

Multiplication
times
in all
total
each

Division
each
equal
per
separate

 Katrina recycles soda cans. She recycled 36 cans last month. This month she recycled 34 cans. How many total cans did she recycle?

 Bradley mailed 22 birthday party invitations. Only 18 friends came to his party. How many friends did not come?

 Jake is 4 years old. His brother, John, is 4 times as old as Jake. How old is John?

 Ramona is going to the carnival. She has $10.00 to buy ride tickets. Each ride ticket costs $2.00. How many ride tickets will she be able to buy?

14

Add or Multiply.

Solve these + and x problems.
Label your answer. Look for key words to help you.

Key Words	Addition		Multiplication	
	additional	in all	times	in all
	altogether	total	total	each
	all	another		

How many total keychains did Gary make for his classmates? He made 16 keychains for the boys and 15 keychains for the girls.

Caroline wants to buy 6 new pairs of socks. Each pair costs $1.50. How much will the 6 new pairs of socks cost?

Scott went on vacation. He put 5 shirts, 5 pairs of pants, 2 jackets, and 2 pairs of shoes into his suitcase. How many total items were in his suitcase.

Peter drove 9 miles to reach his grandfather's house. Peter's brother, Tim, drove 4 times as many miles to get there. How many miles did Tim drive to reach his grandfather's house?

Today, Mrs. Cady's fourth grade class is going on a field trip. No students are absent today. They are assembled in 2 lines. Each line has 12 students. How many total students are in Mrs. Cady's fourth grade class?

Multiply or Divide.

Key Words

Multiplication		Division	
times	in all	each	equal
total	each	per	separate

Solve the problems below using the 4 Step Method.

 Pedro has 63 pieces of candy in a bag. He wants to separate the pieces equally into 7 smaller bags. How many pieces will be in each bag?

 Molly drives 8 miles to work. She works 5 days a week. How many total miles does she drive to work each week?

 Sarah's soccer team will play 6 games in June, 6 games in July, and 6 games in August. How many total soccer games will her team play?

 Mike fills the tank of his car with 9 gallons of gas. He can drive 90 miles before the tank becomes empty. How many miles can he drive on each gallon of gas?

 Gil bought 24 packages of raisins. He ate 2 packages a day until they were all gone. How many days did Gil have raisins to eat?

Solving Word Problems

Addition		**Subtraction**	
additional	in all	difference	left
altogether	total	take away	only
all	another	more than	less than

Multiplication		**Division**	
times	in all	each	equal
total	each	per	separate

Solve the problems below using the 4 Step Method.

Mom is in the kitchen trying to catch a spider. It will jump away 4 times before she catches it. The spider will jump 12 inches, 17 inches, 15 inches, and 18 inches. How many total inches will the spider jump?

Bill has just started collecting baseball cards. He has collected 22 cards so far. He is saving his money to buy more cards. In one year, he will have 12 times as many cards as he now has. How many baseball cards will he have in one year?

Two lemon trees grow in Perry's backyard. He picked 121 lemons last week. This week he picked only 98 lemons. How many more lemons did he pick last week?

Lucinda has 67 logs to use toward building a cabin. She will need another 24 logs before she finishes. How many logs will she use altogether?

Four students collected bugs for a fifth grade science project. They collected a total of 36 bugs. Each student collected an equal number of bugs. How many bugs did each student collect?

17

Tonya bought 27 items at the grocery store. They were packed equally into 3 bags. How many items were in each bag?

Jackie received a Hot Wheels carrying case with 50 Hot Wheel cars in it. She shared 28 cars with her friend Matt. How many cars were left in the carrying case?

Three girls want to buy a large pizza for lunch. Each girl has $6.50. How much money do they have altogether?

Samantha has 60 books. She wants to put them onto 6 shelves. Each shelf will hold the same number of books. How may books will be placed on each shelf?

Last Monday, it rained for 127 minutes. Today it rained for 89 minutes. How much longer did it rain last Monday?

Harriet and her great-grandfather share birthdays. Harriet has just turned 13 years old. Her great-grandfather is 7 times as old as she is. How old is her great-grandfather?

Key Words

Addition
additional
in all
altogether
total
all
another

Subtraction
difference
left
take away
only
more than
less than

Multiplication
times
in all
total
each

Division
each
equal
per
separate

 Ryan bought his mother a bouquet of flowers. The bouquet had 6 roses, 12 carnations, and 5 daffodils. In addition, it had 7 lillies, 11 pansies, and 4 violets. How many total flowers did the bouquet have?

 Charlotte is driving with her family to her grandparent's home. Her grandparents live 243 miles away. Charlotte and her family will stop for lunch after driving 157 miles. How many more miles must she still travel to reach her grandparents?

 Four friends are walking on a very hot day. They stop at a market and buy a 32 ounce drink. How many ounces will each friend drink if they share the drink equally?

 Oops! Steve dropped a box of Raisin Rice Pops Cereal on the floor and most of the cereal spilled out. He picked up 84 raisins and 107 rice pops and threw them all away. How many raisins and rice pops were thrown away altogether?

 The Simi Valley Thanksgiving Parade included 224 people this year. Next year, there will be 3 times as many people in the parade. How many people will be in the parade next year?

The Wilkinson Senior Center has 63 residents. Ms. Calhoun, the center's director, requested young volunteers on Mondays, Wednesdays, and Fridays to keep residents company. She would like 1 volunteer for 7 residents. How many volunteers will be needed each day?

 Cups are on sale at the market. A set of 10 cups costs $4.89. What would be the cost of 3 sets of cups?

 The total number of fifth graders at Grant School is 80. The school has 4 fifth-grade classrooms. If each class has an equal number of students, how many students does each class have?

 Frances bought 3 cases of soft drinks. Each case contained 12 drinks. How many drinks did she buy in all?

 The boss asked Dennis to separate 100 marbles into groups of 20. Each group was to be put into a small bag. If he does the job correctly, how many bags will he use?

 Pam has 9 computer games. Karla has 3 times as many computer games. How many computer games does Karla have?

Charts and Graphs.

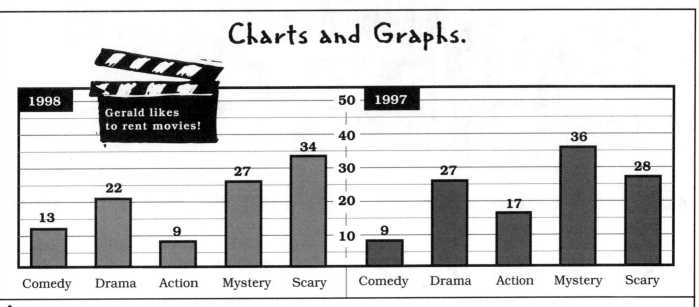

How many total videos did Gerald rent in 1998?

This year Gerald will rent 3 times as many action videos as he rented in 1998. How many action videos will he rent this year?

How many fewer mystery videos did Gerald rent in 1998 than in 1997?

How many total action and drama videos did Gerald rent in 1997?

This year Gerald will rent 32 comedy videos. How many more comedy videos will he rent this year than in 1998?

Hardwall Hardware sells machine bolts by the pack. Harvey wants to buy 150 machine bolts. Each bolt must be 1/2 inch long. He will not buy any packs of 25 machine bolts. How much will Harvey spend?

Shane is building a storage shed in the backyard. He will need to buy 2 boxes of nails. One box will have 100 2-inch nails and the other will have 100 1-inch nails. How much will the 2 boxes of nails cost?

Patty will use 25 pieces of wood to build a table. She bought 1 box of 1 1/2-inch wood screws that cost $2.89. She will put an equal number of wood screws in each piece of wood. When she is finished, no wood screws will remain. How many wood screws will Patty use with each piece of wood?

Larry needed 79 washers to complete a project. He bought a box of washers for $1.19. How many washers did he have left once the project was finished?

Emily needs 1-inch nails. To make sure she has enough, she buys 3 boxes. How many total nails will she have?

Finding Extra Information.

Word problems can have more information than is needed to solve the problem.

> The bookstore is having a big sale! Kayla wants to buy a number of books: 6 mystery books, 4 cooking books, 3 music books, 2 computer books, and 6 children's books. She will give the 6 children's books to her son's teacher. Each book will cost $1.50. How many total books will she buy?

The problem asks: How many total books will she buy?

Important facts: 6 mystery books, 4 cooking books, 3 music books, 2 computer books, and 6 children's books.

Extra information: She will give the 6 children's books to her son's teacher.
Each book will cost $1.50.

Read each problem. Circle the important facts. Draw a line through any extra information. Solve the problem. Label your answer.

Like this

The bookstore is having a big sale! (Kayla wants to buy) a number of books: (6 mystery books, 4 cooking books, 3 music books, 2 computer books, and 6 children's books.) ~~She will give the 6 children's books to her son's teacher. Each book will cost $1.50.~~ How many total books will she buy?

```
  6
  4
  3
  2
+ 6
─────
 21 books
```

Mary works at a fast food restaurant. She works 6 hours on Monday, Tuesday, Thursday, and Saturday. Each day, she grills hamburgers for 4 hours and runs a cash register for 2 hours. How many hours does Mary grill hamburgers in a week?

Zak is on vacation. He has already taken 22 pictures. He has enough film left to take 48 more pictures. If he only takes 37 more pictures, how many total pictures will he have taken on his vacation?

Tony's mother is making 6 fruit cobblers. She will use 4 apples and 36 cherries. Each apple will be cut into 9 slices. Each cherry will be cut in half. Each fruit cobbler will have an equal number of apple slices. How many apple slices will each fruit cobbler have?

Mr. and Mrs Gordon have 6 children. They have 4 boys and 2 girls. Mrs. Gordon wants to buy 3 large pizzas for dinner. Two pizzas will be cheese and the other will be pepperoni. Each pizza will be cut into 10 slices. Each of the boys will eat 4 slices of pizza. How many total slices of pizza will the boys eat?

Pablo has a total of 48 models in his collection. Last Friday, he showed his new friend Sean 6 of these models. He also went to the hobby store and looked at 4 other models. He keeps his models on 8 shelves in his room. Each shelf has an equal number of models. How many models are on each shelf?

Pam likes to read the newspaper. She usually reads the first 6 articles in the Sports Section, the Viewer's Section, the Life Section, and the Business Section. This morning she had time to read 4 articles in the Sports Section, 3 in the Viewer's Section, 4 in the Life Section, and 2 in the Business Section. How many articles did she read altogether this morning?

Kristen and Michael are going to the recycling center to recycle pop cans. Kristen has 67 diet cola cans, and Michael has 54 assorted cans. The recycling center will pay $1.00 for each pound of cans recycled. How many total cans will Kristen and Michael recycle?

Cheryl has tickets to 24 basketball games. She has 2 tickets to each game. She wants to take her friend, Stacey, to 12 of the games. She wants to take her brother to the remaining 12 games. How many basketball tickets does she have altogether?

Scout Troop 522 is going on a 36-mile hike. The scouts want to hike an equal number of miles each day and complete the hike in only 6 days. Each scout will carry a backpack that weights 25 pounds. How many miles will the scouts hike each day?

John bought 32 potatoes at the market. He hopes to use 14 for mashed potatoes and to bake the remaining 18 potatoes. If he really only uses a total of 25 potatoes for mashing and baking, how many potatoes will not be used?

Scott is at the hair salon for a haircut. Seven people are in line ahead of him for the next available haircutter. He sees 9 children, 4 women, and 5 men having their haircut. Altogether, how many people are having their haircut?

Exactly 100 swimmers will try out for the swimming team. The pool is 25 meters long, but each swimmer must swim 100 meters. The pool has 5 lanes. How many sets of races must take place for all swimmers to try out?

The Holymer Pen and Pencil Company must ship 48 boxes of pencils and 63 boxes of pens. The shipping clerk, James, will put 36 of the boxes onto one truck and 75 boxes onto another truck. The trucks will deliver their loads to different stores. How many fewer boxes of pencils will be shipped than boxes of pen?

Mr. and Mrs. Sims are having a Sweet 16 Birthday Party for their daughter, Judy. A total of 64 people will attend. The Sims will rent 64 chairs, 8 round tables, and 4 square tables. Six people can sit at each round table. Four people can sit at each square table. How many total people will be sitting at round tables.

Last week was very windy. Julio cleaned up the mess in the front yard and put it into 2 large trash bags. Although he didn't count them, Julio cleaned up 342 leaves, 96 pieces of trash, and 157 broken twigs. It took him only one hour. How many more leaves did he pick up than twigs?

Yvette sells 36 different magazines and 12 different newspapers at her newstand. The newstand has 7 shelves to hold all magazines and newspapers. Yvette puts an equal number of magazines on 4 shelves. She also puts an equal number of newspapers on the other 3 shelves. How many different magazines are on each magazine shelf?

Hank is hanging pictures in his apartment. He has 13 heavy pictures. Each will require 2 hooks to hang on the wall. The other 11 pictures will need only 1 hook each to hang on the wall. How many total hooks will Hank use to hang the heavy pictures?

Perry collected money from two friends before going to the Candy Store. He bought 1 Mr. Goodbite candy bar for himself and 2 Buttercrunch candy bars, one for each friend. He still had money left. He bought 1 pack of Tropical Tarts for the three of them to share. How much did Perry pay for the candy bars?

Mr. Baxter is babysitting 5 children. He brought 1 box of Sour Grapes and 1 box of Licorice as treats from the Candy Store. He will give each child the same number of Sour Grapes and Licorice pieces. How many Sour Grapes will each child get?

Meagan has $2.00 in her pocket. She wants to buy a box of Gummi Strips or a Chocolate Delight candy bar. How much money will she have left if she only buys the Gummi strips?

Jack and Shawn go to the Candy Store often. Today, Jack bought 1 box of Fruity Bursts and Shawn bought 1 box of Tropical Tarts. Jack traded 5 of his Fruity Bursts for 5 of Shawn's Tropical Tarts. After dinner, Jack ate 7 pieces of candy? How many pieces of candy were still remaining for Jack?

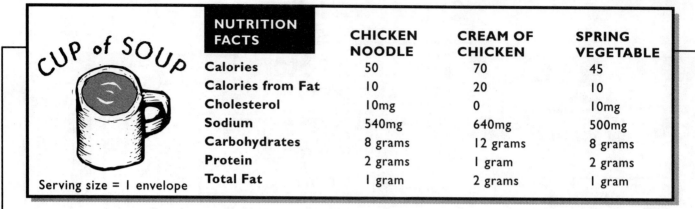

NUTRITION FACTS	CHICKEN NOODLE	CREAM OF CHICKEN	SPRING VEGETABLE
Calories	50	70	45
Calories from Fat	10	20	10
Cholesterol	10mg	0	10mg
Sodium	540mg	640mg	500mg
Carbohydrates	8 grams	12 grams	8 grams
Protein	2 grams	1 gram	2 grams
Total Fat	1 gram	2 grams	1 gram

CUP of SOUP

Serving size = 1 envelope

Nadia was a very hungry girl today. She had 2 cups of chicken noodle soup and 1 cup of spring vegetable. According to the chart, how many total calories were in the 2 cups of chicken noodle soup?

Carol had a cup of cream of chicken soup and only 1/2 cup of chicken noodle soup. How many grams of carbohydrates did Carol get from the chicken noodle soup?

Andy had a hard time deciding which soup to make. He finally decided on the soup with the least number of calories and the least amount of sodium. Which soup did he choose?

For lunch, Sheila is trying to choose between 2 flavors of soup. She doesn't want to have more than 20 milligrams of cholesterol. She has decided to have 1 cup of chicken noodle and 1 cup of spring vegetable. How many total calories will her lunch have?

Problems with Several Steps.

Word problems may require several steps to solve.

The daily special at Harry's Hamburger Hut is a double-cheeseburger, large fries, and a large drink all for $4.59. If the drink is $.65 and the large fries is $1.19, how much does the double-cheeseburger cost?

What does the problem ask? How much does the double-cheeseburger cost?

What are the facts? The daily special is $4.59. The drink is $.65 and the large fries are $1.19.

Like this ➡️

Step 1: Add to find the cost of the drink and the large fries.

```
 .65   drink
+1.19  fries
$1.84  drink & fries
```

Step 2: Subtract to find the cost of the double-cheeseburger alone.

```
 4.59  cost of special
-1.84  cost of drink & fries
$2.75  cost of double-cheeseburger
```

Solve these problems. Label your answer.

 Jeremy is writing a report about Peru. The report has 7 chapters. Four chapters have 3 pages each. The other 3 chapters have 4 pages each. How many pages are in Jeremy's report?

 Wanda is making a keychain for her father. She will use 4 different colors of lanyard material. She will buy 4 yards of each color. If she uses only 3 yards of each color, how many total yards will she have left?

Stephanie works at the Candy Store. She must unpack 3 boxes of chocolate bars. Each box contains 50 individual bars. She needs to unpack 6 boxes of suckers. Each box contains 24 suckers. How many fewer suckers will she unpack than bars?

The Green Jays, a little league baseball team, went to Mario's Pizza Palace. The coach bought 3 large cheese pizzas for the players. Each pizza was cut into 12 pieces. After the team left, 5 pieces of pizza still remained on the table. How many pieces of pizza did the Green Jays eat?

On Monday morning at the local library, 17 books were checked out and 15 books were returned. After lunch, 26 books were returned and 19 books were checked out. How many more books were returned than were checked out?

Karen, Elise, and Sonia are sisters. Their mother bought each child a pair of rollerblades at $59.95 each. She also bought a $19.95 helmet for each child. How much was the total purchase?

Mr. Sutton took his wife and 3 neighbors to the Saturday auto races. He paid a total of $50.00 for admission tickets and 5 sodas. Each soda cost $1.00. How much did each admission ticket cost?

At a Red Cross Disaster Training meeting, the leader divided 48 volunteers into groups of 6 each. Each group was given 3 rolls of tape to practice wrapping wounds. How many total rolls of tape were needed?

The Callahan Family traveled to an amusement park last weekend. Mrs. Callahan paid $20.00 for her admission ticket, $20.00 for her husband's ticket, and another $12.00 for each of their 3 children. She also paid $8.00 to park in the amusement parking lot. What was the cost of the family's admission and parking?

Yesterday morning at National Supermarket, Miguel placed 84 cans of soup next to the 17 cans already on the shelves. At the end of yesterday, only 76 cans of soup were left on the shelves. How many cans of soup were sold yesterday?

Stephanie is the manager of the Loving Hearts Flower Shop. She has 3 delivery people and a total of 17 deliveries to make. She decides to make 2 deliveries herself and to assign an equal number of remaining deliveries to her other people. How many deliveries will each delivery person make?

Hanako is a skater. She wants to skate in the Winter Olympics. She practices 4 hours each Monday, Wednesday, and Friday. She also practices 3 hours on Thursday and Saturday. How many total hours does she practice each week?

Danielle will be 39 years old in 6 years. Her sister Suzanne is 7 years younger. How old will Suzanne be in 5 years?

Tim can speed read two 100-page books in only 110 minutes. Amanda can read one 100-page book in 62 minutes. If Tim and Amanda each read two 100-page books, how much less time will it take Tim to read his books than for Amanda to read her books?

Stacy's mother is serving a chicken dinner to 16 people. Each package of chicken she buys at the market has 4 pieces. How many packages must she buy to make sure that each person has at least two pieces?

Twelve passengers got on the bus at Drummond Street. There were already 5 passengers on board. The bus then stopped at Hillview Lane and another 6 passengers got on while 4 passengers left the bus. Finally, the bus stopped at Nordhoff Street where 7 passengers got on and 15 got off. How many passengers remained on the bus after the last stop.

For years, Laurie drove alone to work 5 days a week. Now her friend Larry carpools to work with her. Together, they use Laurie's car 3 times a week and Larry's car 2 times a week. The trip to work and back uses 2 gallons of gas. How many gallons of gas does Laurie save by driving only 3 times a week instead of 5 times?

More with Charts and Signs

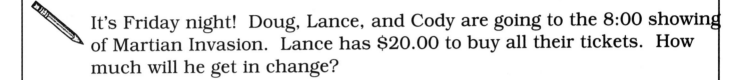

Town Center Theater

	SATURDAY & SUNDAY MATINEES Admission $5.00 tax included			EVENINGS Admission $6.50 tax included		
MARTIAN INVASION	10:00	12:00	2:00	4:00	6:00	8:00
SUMMER HEAT	10:30	1:00	3:30	6:00	8:30	11:00
BASEBALL QUEENS	10:00	12:00	2:00	4:00	6:00	8:00
TERM LIMITS	9:30	12:00	2:30	5:00	7:30	10:00

Gift Certificates $5.00 each, or a book of 5 for $25.00 tax included

It's Friday night! Doug, Lance, and Cody are going to the 8:00 showing of Martian Invasion. Lance has $20.00 to buy all their tickets. How much will he get in change?

Michael loves the movies, so his uncle gave him one book of gift certificates. If his uncle had purchased individual tickets for evening shows, how much more would he have paid?

Saul and June are going to the matinee showing of Summer Heat. Saul has a book with free certificates. How many certificates will he use to get their tickets?

Peter and Carla are going to Martian Invasion on Saturday. They can see the 4:00 showing or the 12:00 matinee. Together, how much will they save by seeing the matinee rather than the 4:00 showing?

DOUGHNUTS ~ COFFEE ~ ETC. !

"We proudly serve cheap, store bought coffee"

CRESCENTS
Butter $1.75
Chocolate 2.25
One Dozen(12) . . 19.95

DOUGHNUTS
Plain . . . . $ .39
Glazed 49
One Dozen(12) . . .5.00

(Prices include tax)

HOT CHOCOLATE
small . . . . . . $ .69
large 99

COFFEE
small 99
large 1.29

MILK 89
JUICE 99

James bought 2 plain doughnuts, 1 glazed doughnut, and a small hot chocolate. What did he pay?

Shirley wants a chocolate crescent and a large coffee. Diane wants 2 glazed doughnuts and a milk. How much more will Shirley pay than Diane?

Mike bought 2 dozen doughnuts to feed 5 hungry people. One person ate 4 doughnuts. The other 4 people divided the remaining doughnuts equally between themselves. How many doughnuts did each of the four people receive?

Carolyn wants to buy 1 chocolate crescent, 1 plain doughnut, and a large coffee. She has $2.45 in her pocket. Luckily, she has more money in her wallet. How much more money will she need from her wallet to make her purchase?

Peter had a business meeting this morning. He bought 3 dozen butter crescents and 2 dozen doughnuts before going to the meeting. How much more did he pay for the butter crescents than the doughnuts?

Post Test

Use after completing pages 13-21

Carissa has 17 dolls. Vanessa has 16 dolls. How many dolls do they have altogether?

- ○ 35 dolls
- ○ 33 dolls
- ○ 31 dolls

Elena mailed 27 holiday greeting cards. She put a $.33 stamp on each card before putting it in the mailbox. How much did it cost to mail all the cards?

- ○ $8.19
- ○ $8.81
- ○ $8.91

Madeline had a bag of 76 pretzels. After eating 39 pretzels, how many did she still have?

- ○ 37 pretzels
- ○ 39 pretzels
- ○ 36 pretzels

Mr. Finch has 24 students in his fourth grade class. He wants to split the students into 4 equal groups. How many students will be in each group?

- ○ 8 students
- ○ 6 students
- ○ 5 students

Lupe is 17 years old. Her great-grandmother is 4 times as old as Lupe. How old is Lupe's great-grandmother?

- ○ 68 years old
- ○ 78 years old
- ○ 58 years old

Post Test

Use after completing pages 22-27.

Milo bought a $1.29 hamburger, a small $.75 order of fries, and a $.99 drink at the Hamburger Hut. What was the total cost of the hamburger and drink?

- ○ $2.28
- ○ $2.88
- ○ $3.28

Shawna bought a box of 24 computer floppy disks for $21.95. She divided them into 4 separate groups and put them into a file drawer. How many disks were in each group?

- ○ 4 floppy disks
- ○ 5 floppy disks
- ○ 6 floppy disks

Amir is shopping for light bulbs. He can buy a box of 2 bulbs for $1.29, or he can buy a box of 4 for $2.35. He decides to buy three boxes at the $2.35 price. How many bulbs will he buy?

- ○ 9 bulbs
- ○ 12 bulbs
- ○ 6 bulbs

Kayla has 122 pennies and 72 nickles. Her friend Marlene has 88 pennies and 81 nickles. How many fewer pennies does Marlene have than Kayla?

- ○ 24 pennies
- ○ 32 pennies
- ○ 34 pennies

Herb went to the pet store. He counted 24 brown rabbits, 22 black rabbits, and 36 white rabbits. The black rabbits and the brown rabbits sold for $21.95 each. The white rabbits sold for only $19.95 each. How many total rabbits did Herb count in the pet store?

- ○ 82 rabbits
- ○ 72 rabbits
- ○ 92 rabbits

Post Test

Use after completing pages 28-33.

Wallace went to the post office and bought 40 stamps. He used 8 stamps to mail letters. He will use 6 stamps tomorrow and 7 stamps the next day. How many stamps will he still have left?

○ 18 stamps
○ 29 stamps
○ 19 stamps

Trisha bought 13 cookies at the school bake sale. Her brother Paul bought 15 cookies at the bake sale. Before going home, Trisha ate 3 of her cookies. Paul ate 3 times as many cookies as his sister. How many more cookies did Trisha have left than Paul?

○ 4 cookies
○ 5 cookies
○ 3 cookies

Marylou took 72 pictures on her vacation. She did not like the way 24 turned out. She wanted to place the remaining pictures in her photo album. She put 6 pictures on each page. How many pages did she use?

○ 7 pages
○ 8 pages
○ 6 pages

Martha is a truck driver. This morning she will deliver 12 packages to a market, 35 packages to a toy store, and 18 packages to a clothing store. This afternoon she will pick up a total of 91 packages. How many fewer packages will she deliver than pick up today?

○ 36 packages
○ 16 packages
○ 26 packages

Jerome is reading a story that is 43 pages long. He will read 9 pages over 4 nights. How many pages will remain after the 4 nights?

○ 8 pages
○ 7 pages
○ 9 pages

Page 5.
75 50 60 33 76 40
43 90 46 93 68 86
53 92 58 71 43 35
51 87 62 70 43 83
90 36 42 64 62 51

Page 6.
59 25 47 37 63 45
59 33 35 55 47 18
58 67 35 73 24 69
12 17 26 66 29 56
46 75 12 34 65 23

Page 7.
54   75   92   70   98   84
264 432 195 243 108 340
72   78   235 105 152   91
265 602 114 570 774 300
38   64   144 225   84   296

Page 8.

1	2	3	4	5	6	7	8
6	5	3	3	4	10	8	5
11	12	10	8	10	3	11	10
9	2	4	2	3	12	9	2
12	8	11	10	9	2	12	8
7	7	1	1	1	6	7	11
8	4	12	12	12	9	10	3
3	11	8	4	2	1	7	9
8	1	5	11	11	8	11	1
12	9	9	5	8	4	10	12
7	6	6	7	6	11	5	4
9	3	7	9	5	5	12	7
6	10	2	6	7	7	9	6

Page 9.
1.69   3.41   5.37 7.25 4.57
6.75   .89   .53   2.96 3.01
6.04   5.39   .77
7.07   12.86 4.27
4.92   .73   .52
2.216   32.48 .746

Page 10.
22.2   3.28   .185 25.2   .126
14.8   33.0   16.8 .228   21.6
43.0   1.02   8.5   .018   18.6
.42   42.7   15.2 1.52   5.13

Pages 11.
Katrina recycles soda cans. She recycled 36 cans last month. This month she recycled 34 cans.
How many total cans did she recycle?

Bradley mailed 22 birthday party invitations. Only 18 friends came to his party.
How many friends did not come?

Pam made fruit salad. She cut a watermelon into 57 pieces. She cut a cantaloupe into 38 pieces.
She cut a honeydew melon into 41 pieces. How many pieces of fruit were in the fruit salad altogether?

Jake is 4 years old. His brother, John, is 4 times as old as Jake.
How old is John?

Ramona is going to the carnival. She has $10.00 to buy ride tickets. Each ride ticket costs $2.00.
How many ride tickets will she be able to buy?

Pages 12.
Katrina recycles soda cans. (She recycled 36 cans last month.) (This month she recycled 34 cans)
How many total cans did she recycle?

(Bradley mailed 22 birthday party invitations.) (Only 18 friends came to his party.)
How many friends did not come?

Pam made fruit salad. (She cut a watermelon into 57 pieces.) (She cut a cantaloupe into 38 pieces.)
(She cut a honeydew melon into 41 pieces.) How many pieces of fruit were in the fruit salad altogether?

(Jake is 4 years old.) His brother, (John, is 4 times as old as Jake.)
How old is John?

Ramona is going to the carnival. (She has $10.00 to buy ride tickets.) (Each ride ticket costs $2.00.)
How many ride tickets will she be able to buy?

Pages 13.
Katrina recycles soda cans. (She recycled 36 cans last month.) (This month she recycled 34 cans)
How many [total] cans did she recycle?

(Bradley mailed 22 birthday party invitations.) ([Only] 18 friends came to his party.)
How many friends did not come?

Pam made fruit salad. (She cut a watermelon into 57 pieces.) (She cut a cantaloupe into 38 pieces.)
(She cut a honeydew melon into 41 pieces.) How many pieces of fruit were in the fruit salad [altogether]?

(Jake is 4 years old.) His brother, (John, is 4 [times] as old as Jake.)
How old is John?

Ramona is going to the carnival. (She has $10.00 to buy ride tickets.) ([Each] ride ticket costs $2.00.)
How many ride tickets will she be able to buy?

 # Answers.

Page 14
70 cans
4 friends
16 years old
5 tickets

Page 15
31 keychains
$9.00
14 items
36 miles
24 students

Page 16
9 pieces
40 miles
18 games
10 miles
12 days

Page 17
62 inches
264 baseball cards
23 lemons
91 logs
9 bugs

Page 18
9 items
22 cars
$19.50
10 books
38 minutes
91 years old

Page 19
45 flowers
86 miles
8 ounces
191 raisins & rice pops
672 people

Page 20
9 volunteers
$14.67
20 students
36 drinks
5 bags
27 computer games

Page 21
105 videos
27 action videos
9 fewer mystery videos
44 action & drama videos
19 more comedy videos

Page 22
$4.47
$6.98
4 wood screws
21 washers
300 nails

Page 23
16 hours
59 pictures

Page 24
6 apple slices
16 slices
6 models
13 articles
121 cans

Page 25
48 tickets
6 miles
7 potatoes
18 people
20 sets

Page 26
15 fewer boxes
48 people
185 leaves
9 different magazines
26 hooks

Page 27
$3.57
5 Sour Grapes
$.65
13 pieces

Page 28
100 calories
4 grams
Spring Vegetable Soup
95 calories

Page 29
24 pages
4 yards

Page 30
6 suckers
31 pieces
5 books
$239.70
$9.00

Page 31
24 rolls
$84.00
25 cans
5 deliveries
18 hours

Page 32
31 years old
7 minutes less
8 packages
11 passengers
4 gallons

Page 33
$5.00
$7.50
2 gift certificates
$3.00

Page 34
$1.96
$1.67
5 doughnuts
$1.48
$49.85

Page 35
33 dolls
$8.91
37 pretzels
6 students
68 years old

Page 36
$2.28
6 floppy disks
12 bulbs
34 pennies
82 rabbits

Page 37
19 stamps
4 cookies
8 pages
26 packages
7 pages